Hajj & Umrah for Beginners

By
Shaykh Mufti Saiful Islām

JKN Publications

© Copyright by JKN Publications

First Published in July 2016

ISBN 978-1-909114-20-3

British Library Cataloguing in Publication Data
A catalogue record for this book is available from the British Library.

All Rights Reserved. No part of this book may be reproduced, stored in a re-
trieval system or transmitted in any form or by any means, electronic, mechani-
cal, photocopying, recording or otherwise, without the prior permission of the
copyright owner.

Publisher's Note:

Every care and attention has been put into the production of this book. If however, you find any errors, they are our own, for which we seek Allāh's ﷻ forgiveness and the reader's pardon.

Published by:

JKN Publications
118 Manningham Lane
Bradford
West Yorkshire
BD8 7JF
United Kingdom

t: +44 (0) 1274 308 456 | w: www.jkn.org.uk | e: info@jkn.org.uk

Book Title: Hajj & Umrah for Beginners

Author: Shaykh Mufti Saiful Islām

"In the Name of Allāh, the Most Beneficent,
the Most Merciful"

Contents

Introduction

In the name of Allāh ﷻ the Most Gracious, the Most Merciful.

Praise be to Allāh ﷻ, the Lord of the worlds and may peace and blessings be upon His Final Messenger, Muhammad ﷺ, upon his noble family, his Companions and upon those who follow their path until the final hour.

This brief but comprehensive book is presented to you to explain the method of performing Hajj, Umrah and Ziyārah.

It was a couple of years ago, when Allāh ﷻ gave me the golden opportunity to perform Hajj with some of my friends and colleagues. After the Hajj period, they encouraged me to compile a book on Hajj in English which will cater for the English speaking audience and assist the first time pilgrims with the basic requirements in regards to the method of performing Hajj, Umrah and Ziyārat.

Even though there are many books on Hajj, the topic of Hajj is in itself so vast that every person's experiences and needs are different.

In this book, I have briefly concentrated on the five days of Hajj and the rituals of performing Umrah and Ziyārah in simple easy English. I have also mentioned some important points which will be beneficial for the pilgrim. I have tried to present the Masāil of Hajj, Umrah and Ziyārah in an extremely simplified manner and at the same time maintaining the balance in so far as the Masāil of Hajj, Umrah and Ziyārah are concerned.

I hope by the grace of Allāh ﷻ that this book becomes a guide for the first time pilgrims as well as a refresher for those who are undertaking Hajj after some time.

May Allāh ﷻ accept this humble effort and make it a means of salvation for this humble servant, his parents, teachers, family, friends, students and the Muslim Ummah at large. Āmeen.

(Shaykh Mufti) Saiful Islām
Principal of JKN
Editor of Al-Mumin Magazine
July 2016/ Ramadhān 1437

Upon Whom Hajj is Fardh (Compulsory)

Hajj literally means to intend. In Shari'ah, it means to visit the sacred house of Allāh ﷻ in Makkah during the months of Hajj, beginning from the 1st of Shawwāl, and to prolong the stay in order to perform particular rituals during the actual days of Hajj: the 8th, 9th, 10th, 11th and 12th of Dhul-Hijjah.

This is the fifth of the religious duties (pillars) of a Muslim which is Fardh on every adult, male and female. It has to be performed once in a lifetime. The conditions that make Hajj Fardh are as follows:

1.   To be a Muslim.
2.   To be mentally fit (not insane).
3.   To be physically fit (not disabled).
4.   Maturity (to be physically mature).
5.   To have sufficient provisions for dependants for the duration of absence, to possess all requirements for travel and be financially independent.
6.   To have security (of route).
7.   A woman must be accompanied by her husband or a Mahram (a male member of her family whom she cannot marry according to Islamic Law).

If any of the above mentioned conditions are not found, Hajj will not be considered Fardh.

When the conditions that make Hajj Fardh are present, then it becomes compulsory upon the person to perform Hajj immediately (during the first available Hajj period). One is not permitted to delay the Hajj as he/she will be committing a major sin.

Our beloved Prophet ﷺ said,

"Hasten in performing Hajj, for verily one will never know what will befall him."

He said,

"The one who intends performing Hajj, must verily hasten."
(Abū Dāwood)

In the Holy Qur'ān, Allāh ﷻ said,

وَلِلّٰهِ عَلَى النَّاسِ حِجُّ الْبَيْتِ مَنِ اسْتَطَاعَ إِلَيْهِ سَبِيلًا وَمَنْ كَفَرَ فَإِنَّ اللّٰهَ غَنِيٌّ عَنِ الْعَالَمِيْنَ

"Hajj (Pilgrimage) to the House of Allāh (the Ka'bah) is a duty that people who are able to find a way there, owe to Allāh (therefore, Muslims who can afford to go to Makkah to perform Hajj have to do so). Whoever rejects (this obligation) then (it should be borne in mind that) surely Allāh is Independent of the entire universe (Allāh is not in need of man's worship. Man benefits himself only by worshipping Allāh)." (3:97)

9

In another verse, Allāh ﷻ states,

وَأَتِمُّوا الْحَجَّ وَالْعُمْرَةَ لِلّٰهِ

"Perform Hajj and Umrah for Allāh." (2:196)

The Holy Prophet ﷺ said, "For an accepted Hajj, there is no reward besides Jannah (Paradise)." (Bukhāri, Muslim)

Sayyidunā Abū Hurairah ؓ reports that the Holy Prophet ﷺ said,

"Whoever performs Hajj for the sake of pleasing Allāh ﷻ and therein utters no word of evil nor commits any sin, shall return from it as free from sin as he was on the day in which his mother gave birth to him."
(Bukhāri, Muslim)

Sayyidunā Abū Hurairah ؓ reports that the Holy Prophet ﷺ said, "An Umrah is an expiation of the sins committed until the next Umrah, while an accepted Hajj is not rewarded except with Paradise."
(Bukhāri, Muslim)

Preparation

1. Ensure that you have arranged to travel with an approved Hajj and Umrah tour operator or with someone who is reliable and has experience in Hajj and Umrah. Aim to travel with those who are pious and God-fearing. If there are scholars present in the group, then it is much more beneficial as their knowledge and guidance will help make the journey of Hajj and Umrah more fruitful.

2. Make sure all your injections have been given as a certificate will be required to get your Hajj visa. Consult your doctor for the correct vaccinations.

3. Travel with a valid passport

4. It is advisable to study a reliable book on Hajj and Umrah and also seek counsel for practical tips from ones Hajj/Umrah group. Try to attend seminars on performing Hajj which normally takes place in the Masājid around the U.K.

5. Pay all your debts before proceeding for Hajj or make adequate arrangements for their repayment.

6. Travel light, as most items can be purchased from either Makkah or Madeenah, so take only the necessary items.

7. If you are on a special medication, make sure you have enough medication.

8. Do not forget to have your utility bills etc paid in your absence or have alternative arrangements made.

9. Ask for forgiveness from family, relatives and friends for your shortcomings and forgive anyone who has wronged you.

Prior to Departure

Before leaving from home, it is recommended to take a proper bath after removing all unwanted hair from the body and clipping the nails. Apply perfume and perform all those acts of hygiene which are forbidden in Ihrām, prior to entering it.

Ensure that you have packed all necessary items appropriately. For example, medications and similar things you would need urgently should be packed in your cabin luggage as your hold baggage might be delayed.

If you are travelling to Makkah first, you must keep your Ihrām with you in your cabin luggage as you will pass the Meeqāt (boundary for Ihrām) before you retrieve your hold baggage.

When in the state of Ihrām, soreness of the inner thighs is very common. Hence, take unscented vaseline with you to prevent this discomfort.

It is Sunnah to perform two Rak'ats of Salāh before departure. On completing the two Rak'ats, thank Allāh ﷻ for the favours He has bestowed upon you by giving you the golden opportunity to embark on this holy mission. Thereafter, make Du'ā to Allāh ﷻ to make the journey easy for you and to make it full of blessings.

Make sure that you perform your Salāh at the correct times and refrain from the Makrooh times. The Makrooh times are;

1.   After performing Fajr Salāh until approximately 15 minutes after sunrise.
2.   At the time of Zawāl (when the sun is on its zenith) which is around ten minutes before the beginning time of Zuhr Salāh.
3.   After performing Asr Salāh until sunset.

Niyyat (Intention)

A Fardh Hajj is performed only once. Therefore perform it with a sincere intention. Have no ulterior motives, for actions are judged by Allāh ﷻ according to intentions. Our Holy Prophet ﷺ said, "Verily, actions are judged according to intentions and every man is granted what he intends." (Bukhāri, Muslim)

When we decide to perform Hajj, let our intentions be solely to gain Allāh's ﷻ pleasure and to fulfil this Fardh Ibādah and obligation. Let it not be for sightseeing, pleasure, trade, or to gain the title 'Hāji'.

Let us heed to the following Hadeeth of the Holy Prophet ﷺ,
"There will come a time when the wealthy people of my Ummah will perform Hajj merely for pleasure, the middle class for trade, the scholars for show and fame and the poorest class for the sake of begging."

(Ad-Daylami)

May Allāh ﷻ, the most Merciful make us sincere and pious Muslims and protect us from hypocrisy, showing off and pride. Always bear in mind that Ikhlās (sincerity) is of vital importance in all types of worship.

The Journey

Three Types of Hajj

1.   Qirān

In this type of Hajj, the pilgrim enters the state of Ihrām with the intention of performing both Umrah and Hajj. A single Ihrām is adopted for both. On reaching Makkah, the pilgrim first performs Umrah and thereafter he performs Hajj in the same Ihrām. Hence, he will remain in the same Ihrām till the end of Hajj. Hajj Qirān is the most rewarding and virtuous.

2.   Tamattu

In this type of Hajj, a pilgrim enters the state of Ihrām with the intention of performing Umrah only. After the completion of Umrah, this Ihrām is removed and another Ihrām is adopted before the 8th of Dhul-Hijjah with the intention of performing Hajj. Hajj Tamattu is the most practical type and is recommended for the first time goers.

3.   Ifrād

In this type of Hajj, a pilgrim enters the state of Ihrām with the intention of performing Hajj only. He does not combine it with Umrah. After entering the Ihrām, the pilgrim will remain under restrictions until the end of Hajj.

Note: Ihrām is not the name of the special clothes one wears during Hajj. These clothes are just the effect of the Ihrām. Ihrām literally means to put oneself under restrictions and hence, it includes all prohibitions that come into effect when one makes the intention of Umrah/Hajj.

Some people think that once these sheets of Ihrām are worn, they cannot be taken off. This is not correct. Hence, if he changes these sheets of Ihrām, he will not come out of the state of Ihrām. He will come out of the state of Ihrām only when he completes all the essential rites of Hajj/Umrah.

Note: As the vast majority of people perform Tamattu which is easier for everyone, I will hereby explain this particular type of Hajj, thus cover both the Hajj and Umrah.

Ihrām

1. On (or prior to) reaching the Meeqāt, perform Ghusl (bath) if possible, otherwise perform Wudhu. Thereafter, put on the two sheets of Ihrām, one to cover the lower part of the body and the other for the upper part of the body. At this moment, men may apply Itr (perfume). Women should keep their entire bodies covered in their normal clothing.

2. Perform two Rak'āt Nafl with the intention of Ihrām with the headgear on. Remember not to pray your Nafl during Makrooh times. It is preferable to recite Sūrah Al-Kāfiroon in the first Rak'āt and Sūrah Al-Ikhlās in the second Rak'āt.

3. On completing the two Rak'āt, sit bareheaded on the prayer mat and make the intention.

Intention

Niyyat for Hajj Qirān

One who is performing Hajj Qirān (performing Hajj and Umrah in one Ihrām) should make the following intention:

"O' Allāh! I intend to perform Hajj and Umrah. Make them easy for me and accept them from me."

Niyyat for Hajj Tamattu

One who is performing Hajj Tamattu (Hajj and Umrah with two separate Ihrām) should make the following intention:

"O' Allāh! I intend to perform Umrah. Make it easy for me and accept it from me."

Note: Only the intention of Umrah will be made at this point. The intention for Hajj will be made prior to the days of Hajj with a new Ihrām.

Niyyat for Hajj Ifrād

One who is performing Hajj Ifrād (only Hajj) should make the following intention:
"O' Allāh ﷻ! I intend to perform Hajj. Make it easy for me and accept it from me."

After the intention has been made, read the following Du'ā (known as Talbiyah) three times:

$$\text{لَبَّيْكَ ٱللّٰهُمَّ لَبَّيْكَ . لَبَّيْكَ لاَ شَرِيْكَ لَكَ لَبَّيْكَ . اِنَّ الْحَمْدَ وَالنِّعْمَةَ لَكَ وَالْمُلْكَ لاَ شَرِيْكَ لَكَ}$$

'Labbayk Allāhumma Labbayk. Labbayka Lā Shareeka Laka Lab-bayk. In-nal Hamda Wanni'mata Laka Wal Mulk Lā Shareeka Lak.'

"Here I am at Your Service, O' Allāh, here I am. Here I am, no part-ner do You have, here I am. Truly, the Praise and the Favour is Yours and the Sovereignty, no partner do You have."

16

Men should recite these words loudly and women should recite silently. Now read Durood Shareef and make Du'ā for as long as you can. Ihrām becomes complete on:
A.   Making the Niyyat (intention).
B.   Recitation of Talbiyah.

Prohibited Acts Whilst in Ihrām

As soon as one makes the Niyyat and recites the Talbiyah, one is called a Muhrim. A Muhrim must strictly abstain from the following:

1)   Intercourse and everything relating or leading towards it, be it verbal or physical.
2)   Quarrelling and using foul language.
3)   Clipping the nails.
4)   Trimming, clipping or shaving hair from the body.
5)   Males must not wear sewn garments, nor any underwear, gloves or socks. Their heads and faces must not be covered at all times.
6)   Women should not cover their faces. However, in the presence of men, the face will have to be covered in such a manner that the covering does not touch the face.
7)   Do not use perfume, scent and everything that has a fragrance like fragrant soap, food items that have a strong fragrance (fish may be consumed), scented tissues and facial wipes similar to those given on the plane. Also, any strong fragranced sweets that freshen the breath, however one may eat sweets that do not freshen the breath.
8)   Killing lice or any unharmful insects.
9)   Using toothpaste. Unflavoured Miswāk is permissible to use.
10)   For males, wearing footwear of any kind that will cover the central bone of the upper part of the feet.

Permissible Acts Whilst in Ihrām

1)   Changing Ihrām clothes or to remove the sheets of Ihrām to have a shower.
2)   Wearing glasses, rings, hearing aids and watches.
3)   Taking a bath/shower.
4)   Covering oneself including the feet when resting but avoiding the face.
5)   Using Miswāk but no toothpaste.
6)   Wearing a money belt.
7)   Use of injections are allowed for medical reasons.
8)   Clipping a broken nail or extracting a tooth.
9)   Carrying something on your head.
10) Looking into a mirror.
11) Use of odourless Surmah (Kuhl, antimony)
12) Rubing the body gently while taking care that no hair falls off the body. It does not matter if some hair comes off by themselves during washing without you intending it.
13) Applying non-fragrant cream to the wounded area

Umrah

Virtues of Umrah

* An Umrah in Ramadhān is superior to the Umrah performed on other days. If Allāh ﷻ gives the Tawfeeq (strength) to spend the month of Ramadhān in Makkah Mukarramah, then perform as many Nafl Umrahs as you can. The Holy Prophet ﷺ said, "An Umrah performed during Ramadhān is equal (in reward) to performing Hajj with me. " (Muslim)

* The Holy Prophet ﷺ said, "An Umrah is an expiation for the sins committed between it and another Umrah." (Bukhāri, Muslim)

* The performers of Hajj and Umrah are deputations of Allāh ﷻ. If they call Him, He answers them and if they seek His forgiveness, He forgives them. (Ibn Mājah)

* Sayyidunā Abdullāh Ibn Mas'ood ﷺ reports that the Holy Prophet ﷺ said, "Perform Hajj and Umrah one after the other. For surely, they (the Hajj and Umrah) remove poverty and sins just as the furnace removes the dirt off iron, gold and silver." (Tirmizi, Nasai)

Farāidh (Compulsory Acts) of Umrah

The Farāidh of Umrah are:

1) To be in the state of Ihrām (special dressing, Niyyat and Talbiyah)
2) Tawāf that is completed with the intention of Umrah.

Wājibāt of Umrah

1) Sa'ee between Safa and Marwah.
2) Halaq (shaving the hair) or Qasr (trimming the hair).

Makkah Mukarramah

After putting the Ihrām on, you should engage yourself in the remembrance of Allāh ﷻ, Istigfār and reciting the Talbiyah as much as possible until you reach Makkah Mukarramah.

Once you are in Makkah, settled down in the hotel, it is best to take a rest and carry out the basic necessities before going to Masjid-Harām. Before proceeding to Masjid-Harām, perform Wudhu or have a bath.

Note: Remember, Ihrām restrictions apply, therefore only use water and not any fragranced soap or shampoo. Choose an appropriate time to go to the Masjid. Avoid the times which are very close to Salāh times or times of congestion. If you are performing Umrah, it is desirable that you enter from Bābul-Umrah.

When entering the Majid, enter with your right foot and say:

بِسْمِ اللهِ وَالصَّلٰوةُ وَالسَّلَامُ عَلٰى رَسُوْلِ اللهِ اَللّٰهُمَّ رَبِّ اغْفِرْ لِيْ ذُنُوْبِيْ وَافْتَحْ لِيْ اَبْوَابَ رَحْمَتِكَ

Bismillāhi Wassalātu Wassalāmu' Alā Rasoolillāh, Allāhummaghfir Lee Dhunoobi Waftah Lee Abwāba Rahmatik.

20

'In the Name of Allāh. May Peace and Salutations (of Allāh) be upon the Messenger of Allāh. O' Allāh, open for me the doors of Your Mercy.' (Tirmizi)

When you see the Holy Ka'bah, say the following three times:

اَللّٰهُ اَکْبَرُ لَا اِلٰهَ اِلَّا اللّٰه

Allāhu Akbar Lā Ilāha Illallāh

'Allāh is the Greatest. There is no god except Allāh.'

Thereafter, recite Durood Shareef and make as much Du'ā as possible in front of the Holy Ka'bah whilst standing and raising your hands.

This moment is very precious for whatever Du'ā is made is most certainly accepted by Allāh ﷻ. Do remember this humble writer in your Du'ās also.

Tawāf

Tawāf literally means to go around something.' Islamically, it means an act of worship that involves going around the Ka'bah seven times. This is done anti clockwise with the Ka'bah to your left hand side.

Sayyidunā Abdullāh Ibn Abbās ؓ reported that the Holy Prophet ﷺ said, "One hundred and twenty mercies from Allāh ﷻ descend upon the Ka'bah every night and day. Sixty of them are for those performing Tawāf, forty for those who are engaged in Salāh and twenty for those who

21

are merely looking at the Ka'bah!" (Baihaqi)

Tawāf is a Fardh (compulsory) act of Umrah. During Tawāf engage yourself in Du'ā and Dhikr of Allāh ﷻ. The recitation of the Holy Qur'ān is
also permissible. Tawāf has the same requirements as Salāh, in so far as
purity and intention are concerned. One who does not have Wudhu cannot perform Tawāf and Tawāf performed without intention needs to be
repeated.

Note: You must be free from all major impurities in order to perform
Tawāf and to enter the Masjid-Harām. Major impurities are those conditions when one is in need of a compulsory bath.

Note: If one breaks their Wudhu whilst performing Tawāf, one
should immediately go to perform Wudhu in the designated areas of the
Haram and thereafter continue ones Tawāf from where one has left it and
the circuit one left it in. There is no need to commence ones Tawāf again.

Procedure of Tawāf

- Proceed towards the corner of the Ka'bah in which lies the Hajar
  Aswad (Black Stone).
- Stand at a convenient distance from the Ka'bah and facing the Black
  Stone, raise both hands up to the shoulders as done in Salāh and
  say,

$$\text{بِسْمِ اللهِ اَللهُ اَكْبَرُ}$$
Bismillāhi Allāhu Akbar

22

and kiss the hands. This is known as Istilām. It should be performed at the end of every round facing Hajar Aswad.

- After the Istilām, move towards the right keeping the Ka'bah on your left and walk around the Ka'bah anticlockwise until you return to the Black Stone.
- On completing the seventh circuit, perform Istilām for the eighth time.
- Now perform two Rak'ats Wājib Salāh for Tawāf if it is not the Makrooh time. It is best to perform this Salāh behind the Maqām Ibrāheem. However, if there is a crowd then this Salāh can be performed anywhere in the Haram. It is Sunnah to recite Sūrah Kāfiroon in the first Rak'at and Sūrah Ikhlās in the second Rak'at of the Tawāf Salāh.
- After performing the Salāh, make Du'ā and drink the holy water of Zam Zam to your fill.

Duā when drinking Zam Zam water:

$$اَللّٰهُمَّ اِنِّیْ اَسْاَلُكَ عِلْمًا نَّافِعًا وَّرِزْقًا وَّاسِعًا وَّشِفَآءً مِّنْ كُلِّ دَآءٍ$$

**Allāhumma-innee-as'aluka-ilman-nāfi-aw-wa-rizqaw
wāsi-aw-wa-shifā'am-min-kulli-dā-in**

"O Allāh, I ask of You (to give me) beneficial knowledge, ample provisions and restoration from every illness." (Mustadrak Hākim)

23

Masā'il Regarding Tawāf

- Before commencing Tawāf, make Idtibā (covering of the body in a manner that the left shoulder, left arm and back are covered and the right arm is entirely exposed (for men only). Discontinue with the Idtibā after the Tawāf has been completed. The two Rak'at Wājib Salāh should not be performed with the arm exposed (i.e. with Id-tibā)

- In the first three circuits of Tawāf, it is Sunnah to make Ramal (men only). Ramal means to walk hastily, taking short steps and lifting the legs forcefully, keeping the chest out and moving the shoulders simultaneously. One should walk normally in the four remaining circuits.

- Whilst performing Tawāf, one may do any of the following:

1) Recitation of the Holy Qur'ān. However, this should be done quietly so as not to disturb others.
2) Dhikrullāh - Tasbeeh, Tahleel, Takbeer or Durood Shareef.

Note: Tasbeeh is Subhān-Allāh
　　　　Tahleel is Lā Ilāha-Illallāh
　　　　Takbeer is Allāhu Akbar

3) There are no fixed Du'ās for Tawāf. One should rather make Du'ā for the fulfilment of ones needs of both this world and the Here-after.

- It is recommended to recite the following Du'ā during Tawāf,

سُبْحَانَ اللهِ وَالْحَمْدُ لِلهِ وَلَا اِلٰهَ اِلَّا اللهُ وَاللهُ اَكْبَرُ وَلَا حَوْلَ وَلَا قُوَّةَ اِلَّا بِاللهِ

**Subhānallāhi Wal Hamdulillāhi Wa Lā ilāha illallāhu Wallāhu Akbar
Wa Lā Hawla Wa Lā Quwwata illā Billāhi**

**"Glory be to Allāh and Praise be to Allāh and there is none worthy of
worship but Allāh and Allāh is the Greatest and there is no power or
might except with Allāh."** (Ibn Mājah)

- During Tawāf when you come to Rukn Yamāni, merely touch it
  with both hands or the right hand. It is not Sunnah to kiss or raise
  hands at this corner.

- Between Rukn Yamāni and Hajar Aswad, it is Sunnah to recite,

رَبَّنَا اٰتِنَا فِي الدُّنْيَا حَسَنَةً وَّ فِي الْاٰخِرَةِ حَسَنَةً وَّ قِنَا عَذَابَ النَّارِ

**"O 'Allāh, grant us goodness in this world and goodness in the here-
after and save us from the punishment of the Hellfire."**

- It is Makrooh Tahreemi (strongly disliked) to face or turn ones
  back towards the Ka'bah whilst in Tawāf. Facing the Ka'bah is allowed only when one is facing the corner of the Hajar Aswad and
  Rukn Yamāni.

- Hateem is part of the Ka'bah. Therefore, one must go around the
  Hateem to complete the Tawāf.

- It is Mustahab to perform the 9th Istilām before proceeding for Sa'ee.

Sa'ee (To Walk Briskly Between Safā and Marwah)

Sa'ee literally means to walk briskly. It is carried out in the memory of Sayyidah Hājirah's anxious search of water for her son, Ismāeel العليه . In the context of Hajj and Umrah, it is the act of walking briskly between two hills called Safā and Marwah for seven lengths, not circuits.

The area wherein Sa'ee takes place is known as the Mas'ā. It is approximately 400 metres in length. Sa'ee is to walk seven times between this, starting at Safā (the seventh one will end at Marwah).

1) After the Istilām, proceed to Safā (in the direction of the green light on the wall).
2) Climb Safā and then make the Niyyat (intention) for Sa'ee.
3) It is Sunnah to recite the following Du'ā:

لَا اِلٰهَ اِلَّا اللهُ وَحْدَهُ وَشَرِيْكَ لَه لَهُ الْمُلْكُ وَلَهُ الْحَمْدُ وَهُوَ عَلٰى كُلِّ شَيْنٍ قَدِيْرٌ وَلَا اِلٰهَ اِلَّا اللهُ وَحْدَهُ اَنْجَزَ وَعْدَه وَنَصَرَ عَبْدَه وَهَزَمَ الْاَحْزَابَ وَحْدَه

Lā ilāha illal Lāhu Wahdahu Lā Shareekalahu Lahul Mulku Walahul Hamdu Wa huwa Alā Kulli Shayin Qadeer, Lā ilāha illal Lāhu Wahdahu Anjaza Wa'dahu Wa Nasara Abdahu Wa Hazamal Ahzāb Wahdahu

There is no god but Allāh the One Who has no partner. For Him is the Kingdom and for Him is all Praise and He has Power over everything. There is no god but Allāh the One Who fulfilled His promise, assisted His Servant and defeated the groups alone. ' (Muslim)

4)   Each time, it is desirable to make Du'ā facing the Ka'bah at the hill of Safā and the hill of Marwah. During Sa'ee, make Dhikr. There are no fixed Du'ās for Sa'ee. This is also a place where Du'ā is readily accepted, so one should lengthen ones Du'ā here.

5)   Walk from Safā to Marwah with a normal pace. Whilst walking between Safā and Marwah, you should engage yourself in Dhikr and Du'ā.

6)   When you reach the green lights, you should quicken your pace and walk fast until you reach the other set of green lights. Thereafter, you should resume the normal speed of walking till you reach Marwah. Women, however must walk at their normal pace between the green lights. In between the green lights, it is Sunnah to recite:

رَبِّ اغْفِرْ وَارْحَمْ أَنْتَ الْأَعَزُّ الْأَكْرَمُ

Rabbigfir Warham Antal A'azzul-Akram.
"O' my Lord, forgive and have mercy. You are the Most Majestic, the Most Generous." (Ibn Abi Shaibah)

7)   When you reach the hill of Marwah, you will do exactly the same as done at the hill of Safā and make Du'ā. Safā to Marwah is considered as one circuit of Sa'ee. Returning from Marwah to Safā is considered as another circuit. The Sa'ee will end with the seventh cir-

cuit at the hill of Marwah where it is desirable to make a final Du'ā facing towards the Ka'bah.

8) It is Mustahab (desirable) to perform two Rak'ats of Salāh after Sa'ee. This Salāh should be performed in Masjid Harām and not at the hill of Marwah nor at the hill of Safā.

Masā'il Regarding Sa'ee

1) Unlike Tawāf, it is not necessary to be in the state of Wudhu for the Sa'ee to be correct. Therefore, if you do not have Wudhu or Wudhu breaks during the Sa'ee, continue and do not stop the Sa'ee to go to perform Wudhu.

2) You may take rest during Sa'ee or even after Tawāf before commencing Sa'ee.

3) Technically, Mas'ā (the area of Sa'ee) is outside the Masjid. Hence, the rule regarding the Masjid is not applicable here. If a woman menstruates after Tawāf and before Sa'ee, she may perform her Sa'ee in her menses. However, she must enter and leave the Mas'ā from the backdoors and avoid entering into Masjid Harām.

4) It is also not necessary to make intention for Sa'ee. However, if you prefer to make intention, you could make it as follows:

اَللّٰهُمَّ اِنِّیْ اُرِیْدُ السَّعْیَ بَیْنَ الصَّفَا وَالْمَرْوَةِ سَبْعَةَ اَشْوَاطٍ فَیَسِّرْہُ لِیْ وَتَقَبَّلْهُ مِنِّیْ

Allahumma Inni Uridus Sa'ya Bainas Safā wal Marwati Sab'ata Ashwātin Fa Yassirhu Lee Wa Taqqabalhu Minni

"O' Allāh, I am performing Sa'ee of Safā and Marwah seven times. Make it easy for me and accept it from me."

28

Halaq (Shaving of the Head)

1) After the Sa'ee, in order to release the Ihrām, it is Wājib to shave the entire head or to trim to the length of the first joint of the forefinger.

2) Females will not shave their heads. According to Islām, it is unlawful and Harām for them to do so. In order to release herself from the Ihrām, a woman is only permitted to have her hair trimmed.

3) A woman should take the tip of her plait and cut one inch of the hair. If the hair is very fine at the tip of the plait, then that tip should be ignored and the inch for cutting should be measured from further up the plait.

4) Females must have their hair trimmed in privacy and not on the streets or the hairdressers. A non Mahram is not permitted to trim, touch or look at their hair.

5) For males both Halaq and Qasr (trimming) are permissible, but Halaq is much more preferable. The Holy Prophet 🕮 has supplicated thrice for those who shaved and only once for those who trimmed their hair. (Bukhāri)

Note: Even if there is no hair on the head or it is shorter than one inch then to pass the razor or blade over the head is necessary.

6) One can do Halaq or Qasr of ones own head or have it done at any barber's shop, which are found throughout the Haram. A person may also do Halaq or Qasr of another Muhrim's hair when both are in this situation.

After Halaq or Qasr, Umrah is complete and one is free from the state of Ihrām.

29

Note: If one is performing Hajj Qirān after the Umrah, do not do Halaq or Qasr, but stay in the state of Ihrām.

May Allāh ﷻ accept your Umrah and all your supplications. Āmeen

Stay in Makkah

- Whilst staying in Makkah after Umrah, it is highly recommended to perform Nafl Tawāf. This is more superior than to perform Nafl Umrah. Sayyidunā Abdullāh Ibn Abbās ؓ relates that the Holy Prophet ﷺ said, "One hundred and twenty mercies from Allāh ﷻ descend upon the Ka'bah every day and night; sixty for those performing Tawāf, forty for those engaged in Salāh and twenty for those who are merely looking at the Ka'bah." (Baihaqi)
- Remain busy in Salāh, Du'ā and the recitation of the Holy Qur'ān as a good deed in Makkah is equal to 100,000 good deeds elsewhere. The Holy Prophet ﷺ said, "Salāh in my Masjid (Madeenah) has a virtue of 1000 Salāh in any other Masjid besides it apart from Masjid Harām and one Salāh there holds the reward of a hundred Salāh in my Masjid."
- One should avoid all prohibited and disliked acts. Sayyidunā Umar ؓ said, "I would prefer to commit seventy sins at Rukyah (place outside Makkah) than to commit one sin in Makkah."
- Visit the graveyard of Makkah called Al Mu'allā and other sacred places of Makkah.
- Utilise every moment of your time in carrying out good deeds. Do not waste time sitting around doing nothing or walking aimlessly in the shopping malls.
   Remember! You may not get this golden opportunity again.

30

Hajj

Farāidh (Obligatory Acts) of Hajj

1) To come into Ihrām with intention of Hajj and to recite the Talbi-yah.

2) To stay at Arafāt anytime after mid-day on the 9th of Dhul-Hijjah until the beginning time of Fajr on the 10th of Dhul-Hijjah. This stay may be only for a few minutes.

3) To perform Tawāf-e-Ziyārat.

Wājibāt of Hajj

1) The Sa'ee between Safā and Marwah after Tawāf-e-Ziyārat.

2) To stay in Arafāt until sunset.

3) Wuqoof (stay) in Muzdalifah from the dawn of 10th of Dhul-Hijjah until before sunrise.

4) Ramee (pelting) of the Jamarāt.

5) Nahr (animal sacrifice) for the one performing Hajj Qirān or Ta-mattu.

6) Halaq/Qasr (shaving or trimming the hair). Women will only trim one inch.

7) To perform Tawāf-e-Widā (Farewell Tawāf)

The Five Days of Hajj

Important Advice

During the five days of Hajj, there will be a lot of travelling to be done in crowds and heat. Various rituals will be performed at different places and times. Therefore, a good amount of rest should be taken before leaving for Minā which will be on the 8th of Dhul-Hijjah. Take only the things which are essential before you leave for Minā. Minimise the amount of luggage you take, include only essential items.

The following items should be taken to Minā:
- Holy Qur'ān
- Du'ā books
- Hajj Guide books
- Prayer mat
- One additional pair of Ihrām/clothes
- Sleeping blanket
- Medication
- Toiletries
- Snacks
- A small pouch/bag would be useful for collecting pebbles in Muzdalifah
- Mobile phone with charger

Note: A Mutamatti (a person performing Hajj Tamattu) will enter in the state of Ihrām at anytime before the 8th of Dhul-Hijjah with the intention of performing Hajj. If you are performing Hajj Qirān or Ifrād, you will already be in the state of Ihrām. However, if you are performing Tamattu, then you will do the following after Fajr on the 8th of Dhul-Hijjah .

Day 1 - 8th Dhul-Hijjah
Yawmut Tarwiyah

Minā

On this day, you should prepare to travel to Minā after sunrise. Prior to doing so, men should wear their Ihrām. Women do not put on the Ihrām sheets like men. They should wear their normal clothing. Thereafter, you should go to Masjid Harām and perform two Rak'āts Salāh with the intention of entering into the state of Ihrām. One should keep their head covered whilst performing the two Rak'āts. Men should uncover their heads and remain bareheaded until the conditions of Ihrām are lifted. The intention for Hajj can be made in any language, however the following Du'ā can be made:

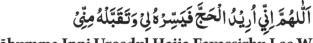

Allāhumma Inni Ureedul Hajja Fayassirhu Lee Wa Taqabbalhu Minnee

"O'Allāh, I intend to perform Hajj. Make it easy for me and accept it from me."

There are two Sunnah acts to be completed in Minā on the 8th of Dhul-Hijjah ;
1) To perform five Salāhs in Minā: Zuhr, Asr, Maghrib and Ishā of the 8th of Dhul-Hijjah and Fajr of the 9th of Dhul-Hijjah .
2) To stay the night in Minā on the 8th of Dhul-Hijjah .

33

Whilst in Minā, one should do the following:

1)   Recite Talbiyah as much as possible.
2)   Stay in constant Dhikr (Remembrance of Allāh ﷻ).
3)   Perform Nafl Salāh.
4)   Engage in reciting the Holy Qur'ān, doing Istighfār and reciting Durood Shareef.

Note: It is Sunnah to leave for Minā on the 8th of Dhul-Hijjah after sunrise as done by our Holy Prophet ﷺ. However, the tour operators usually take the groups after Ishā Salāh, the night before. Please check with your tour operator before leaving.

Mas'alah
When you arrive in Makkah for Hajj, if the total number of days you intend to stay continuously in Makkah before the 8th of Dhul-Hijjah are fifteen days or more, then you are classed as a Muqeem (resident) i.e. you will perform all your Salāhs during the five days of Hajj completely.

However, if you stay less than fifteen days in Makkah, you are a Musāfir (traveler) and therefore, you will make Qasr (shortening Salāh) i.e. perform two Rak'āt Fardh of Zuhr, Asr and Ishā unless you perform your Salāh behind a Muqeem Imām. Similarly, the Qurbāni of Eidul Adhā which is performed annually is also Wājib upon the Muqeem if he possesses the Nisāb of Zakāt but not upon the Musāfir.

The Fast of Arafāt

It is best for the pilgrims not to fast on the day of Arafāt. The Holy Prophet ﷺ did not fast on this day when he performed the farewell Hajj.

Takbeer-e-Tashreeq

Takbeer Tashreeq will be recited immediately after the Fardh Salāh starting from the Fajr of the 9th of Dhul-Hijjah . The Takbeer will be recited once after each Fardh Salāh up to and including Asr Salāh on the 13th of Dhul-Hijjah . The Talbiyah will be recited after the Takbeer-e-Tashreeq from Fajr on the 9th of Dhul-Hijjah .

The Takbeer-e-Tashreeq will be recited as follows:

اَللّٰهُ اَكْبَرُ اَللّٰهُ اَكْبَرُ لَا اِلٰهَ اِلَّا اللّٰهُ وَاللّٰهُ اَكْبَرُ اَللّٰهُ اَكْبَرُ وَلِلّٰهِ الْحَمْدُ

Allāhu Akbar Allāhu Akbar Lā Ilāha Illallāhu Wallāhu Akbar Allāhu Akbar Wa Lillāhil Hamd

Allāh is the Greatest, Allāh is the Greatest, there is none worthy of worship except Allāh and Allāh is the Greatest, Allāh is the Greatest and for Allāh is all Praise.

Men will recite it loudly and women will recite in a soft voice.

Day 2 - 9th Dhul-Hijjah
Yawmul-Arafāt

Perform Fajr Salāh in Minā and prepare to leave for Arafāt which is approximately 9 miles away from Makkah and 6 miles away from Mina.

Do not leave Mina before sunrise as this is against the Sunnah.

Arafāt is the most important day of Hajj. For the Hajj to be valid, one must attend at least a few seconds in Arafāt. This must be anytime between mid-day and the start of Fajr on the 10th of Dhul-Hijjah . If you do not get to Arafāt on this time frame, the Hajj will not be valid.

There is no need to make intention for the stay at Arafāt. A woman does not need to be free from her menstruation. The stay of Arafāt will be valid even though a person is unconscious or sleeps throughout the stay of Arafāt.

Mas'alah
The actual time of Wuqoof (stay) in Arafāt is from Zawāl till sunset. It is Wājib (compulsory) to stay in Arafāt for this period of time.

Once you reach Arafāt, fulfill all your necessities e.g. sleeping, eating and relieving yourself. Perform Wudhu (Ghusl is more preferable if possible). Perform Zuhr Salāh and engage yourself in Ibādah. You may engage in any form of Dhikr, recitation of the Holy Qur'ān and Du'ā between Zuhr and Asr. After Asr Salāh, it is better to engage in Du'ā only. To stand and raise your hands in Du'ā during the stay in Arafāt is Mustahab.

Sayyidah Āisha 🌸 reports that the Holy Prophet 🌸 said, "There is no day in which Allāh 🌸 sets free more souls from the fire of Hell than on the day of Arafat."

The Prophet's 🌸 Sermon on the Farewell Hajj

Before I proceed with the rest of the Masā'il, I would like to mention an extract of the sermon which was delivered by our beloved Prophet 🌸 on the Day of Arafāt, the 9th of Dhul-Hijjah, 10th year of Hijri corresponding to Gregorian year of 632 AD.

"O' people, lend me an attentive ear for I don't know whether after this year I shall be amongst you again. Therefore listen to what I am saying to you carefully and take these words to those who could not be present here today.

O' people, just as you regard this month, this day and this city as sacred, so regard the life and property of every believer as a sacred trust. Return the goods entrusted to you to their rightful owner. Hurt no one so that no one may hurt you. Remember that you will indeed meet your Lord and that He will indeed take account of your deeds.

Allāh 🌸 has forbidden you to take interest, therefore all interest dealings shall be waived.

Beware of Shaytān for the safety of your religion. He has lost all hope that he will ever be able to lead you astray in big matters, so beware of following him in small matters.

37

O' people, it is true that you have certain rights with regard to your women but they also have rights over you. If they abide by your right then to them belongs the right to be fed and clothed in kindness. Treat your women well and be kind to them for they are your partners and true helpers. And it is your right that they do not make friends with anyone of whom you do not approve, as well as never to commit adultery.

O' people, listen to me attentively, worship Allāh, perform your five daily prayers, fast during the month of Ramadhān and give your wealth in Zakāt, perform Hajj if you could afford to.

You know that every Muslim is the brother of another Muslim. You are all equal. Nobody has superiority over another except by piety and good actions. Remember, one day you will appear before Allāh ﷻ and answer for your deeds. So beware! Do not stray from the path of righteousness after I am gone.

O' people, no Prophet or Messenger will come after me and no new faith will be born.

O' people, understand my words which I convey to you. I leave behind me two things; the Holy Qur'ān and the Sunnah and if you follow these, you will never go astray.

All those who listen to me shall pass on my words to others and those to others again and may the last ones understand my words better than those who listen to me directly. Be my witness, O' Allāh ﷻ that I have conveyed Your message to Your people."

I earnestly hope that the group leader or a scholar of each group could read it out to the whole group in Arafāt before performing the Zuhr Salāh.

38

Zuhr Salāh and Asr Salāh in Arafāt

There are two opinions regarding the Zuhr Salāh and Asr Salāh in Arafāt according to the Hanafi school of thought.

1)   Opinion of Imām Abū Haneefah ﷺ

Zuhr and Asr Salāh cannot be combined at the time of Zuhr in the tents. They can only be combined in Masjid Namirah (Masjid in Arafāt) behind the Imām and not in the tents. Therefore, Salāh must be performed in their original times if performed in the tents.

2)   Opinion of Imām Abū Yūsuf ﷺ and Imām Muhammad ﷺ

Zuhr and Asr Salāh can be combined at the time of Zuhr even in the tents. Both opinions are correct. Therefore, do not criticize or argue with anyone who follows a different opinion to yours.

If you choose to follow the first opinion, then straight after midday, perform Zuhr Salāh and at the time of Asr, perform the Asr Salāh. Do not forget to recite the Takbeer-Tashreeq after the Fardh of Zuhr and Fardh of Asr Salāh.

If you choose to follow the second opinion, then straight after mid-day perform the Fardh of Zuhr Salāh. After completing the Fardh of Zuhr, recite the Takbeer-e-Tashreeq. Thereafter, immediately commence your Fardh of Asr Salāh followed by Takbeer-Tashreeq.

Special Du'ā of Arafāt

Our beloved Prophet ﷺ has stated,

"When one reads the following (Du'ā) after Zawāl (mid-day) in Arafāt on the day of Arafāt (9th of Dhul-Hijjah), facing the Qiblah,

100 times fourth Kalimah,

لَا اِلٰهَ اِلَّا اللّٰهُ وَحُدَه وَشَرِيْكَ لَه لَه الْمُلْكُ وَلَه الْحَمْدُ يُحْيِى وَيُمِيْتُ بِيَدِهِ الْخَيْرُ وَهُوَ عَلٰى كُلِّ شَيْءٍ قَدِيْرٌ

Lā ilāha illal Lāhu Wahdahu Lā Shareekalahu Lahul Mulku Walahul Hamdu Yuhyee Wa yumeetu Biyadihil Khair Wa Huwa Alā Kulli Shayin Qadeer

100 times Sūrah Ikhlās,

قُلْ هُوَ اللّٰهُ أَحَدٌ . اَللّٰهُ الصَّمَدُ . لَمْ يَلِدْ وَلَمْ يُوْلَدْ . وَلَمْ يَكُنْ لَّه كُفُوًا أَحَدٌ

Qul Huwallāhu Ahad Allāhus Samad Lam Yalid Wa Lam Yoolad Wa Lam Yakul Lahu Kufuwan Ahad

100 times Durood Ibrāheem.

اَللّٰهُمَّ صَلِّ عَلٰى مُحَمَّدٍ وَعَلٰى اٰلِ مُحَمَّدٍ كَمَا صَلَّيْتَ عَلٰى اِبْرَاهِيْمَ وَعَلٰى اٰلِ اِبْرَاهِيْمَ اِنَّكَ حَمِيْدٌ مَّجِيْدٌ اَللّٰهُمَّ بَارِكْ عَلٰى مُحَمَّدٍ وَعَلٰى اٰلِ مُحَمَّدٍ كَمَا بَارَكْتَ عَلٰى اِبْرَاهِيْمَ وَعَلٰى اٰلِ اِبْرَاهِيْمَ اِنَّكَ حَمِيْدٌ مَّجِيْدٌ

Allāhumma Salli Alā Muhammad Wa Alā Ali Muhammad Kamā Sallayta Alā Ibrāheema Wa Alā Āli Ibrāheema Innaka Hameedum

Majeed. Allāhumma Bārik Alā Muhammad Wa Alā Ali Muhammad Kamā Bārakta Alā Ibrāheema Wa Alā Āli Ibrāheema Innaka Hameedum Majeed

Then Allāh ﷻ says, "O' My Angels! What is the reward for My Servant who glorifies Me, praises Me, mentions My Oneness and Greatness and sends salutations on My Messenger. I will forgive him and accept his request regarding his needs and if My servant intercedes for all who are in Arafāt, I will accept it and he may ask for whatever he wishes."

Mas'alah

There is no Jumuah Salāh in Arafāt. The pilgrims will perform Zuhr Salāh on Friday.

Mas'alah

It is Mustahab (recommended) to engage in Du'ā standing, facing the Qiblah. It is also permissible to sit or lie down if the need arises.

Note: Arafāt is the main place for the acceptance of Du'ā. Repent and perform Du'ā earnestly and in abundance and try to shed tears. Pray for forgiveness for yourself, parents, family, relatives and friends.

Make Du'ā for the Holy Prophet ﷺ, the Sahābah ؓ, pious predecessors, ones teachers and all the Muslims whether they are alive or have passed away.

Pray for global peace, safety and security of our Muslim brothers and sisters. Ask from Allāh ﷻ for all your lawful needs of this world and the Hereafter. Let not laziness or tiredness come near you. Remember that this golden opportunity might not come again, so value each moment properly.

This humble writer (Saiful Islām) requests you to earnestly remember him, his parents, family, teachers, colleagues and students in your Du'ās too.

Mas'alah
To remain in Arafāt until sunset is necessary.

Mas'alah
After sunset, leave for Muzdalifah. Do not perform Maghrib at Arafāt after sunset.

Note: Before you get ready to leave for Muzdalifah, use the toilet facilities as there will be large queues in Muzdalifah.

Muzdalifah

Once you have arrived at Muzdalifah, then immediately perform your Maghrib and Ishā Salāh providing the time for Ishā Salāh has started. If you arrive at Muzdalifah early and the time of Ishā has not started, you will wait until the time of Ishā starts before you can perform these two Salāh. The Maghrib and Ishā Salāh will be performed together at the time of Ishā.

Method of Performing Maghrib and Ishā Combined

When the time for Ishā Salāh commences, perform Maghrib and Ishā Salāh with one Adhān and one Iqāmah as follows:

1) Call out one Adhān.
2) Say Iqāmah.
3) Perform the 3 Rak'ats Fardh of Maghrib Salāh.
4) Then perform the 4 Fardh of Ishā Salāh.
5) Perform the two Rak'ats Sunnah of Maghrib Salāh.
6) Perform the 2 Rak'ats Sunnah of Ishā Salāh.
7) Finally, perform the 3 Rak'ats Witr of Ishā Salāh.

Mas'alah

After Salāh, attend to your needs and thereafter, spend the rest of the night in worship.

Mas'alah

It is Sunnah Mu'akkadah to remain in Muzdalifah until Subah Sādiq and to remain awake in Tilāwat, Du'ā and Ibādah is Mustahab (praiseworthy).

Try to get some sleep also as this is a Sunnah of the Holy Prophet ﷺ. The Holy Prophet ﷺ took a good rest due to the tiredness he had felt during the day of Arafāt and with the intention of getting prepared for the next day.

Note: The Holy Prophet ﷺ has exempted the women, the sick and disabled people from staying the night in Muzdalifah due to the immense crowd, but to avoid unnecessary problems, women should stay the night and depart in the morning after Fajr Salāh with their husband/Mahram.

Collecting Pebbles

Collect pebbles approximately the size of a pea or a date seed to pelt the Jamarāt. You should pick at least 49 pebbles if you are only pelting for 3 days until the 12th of Dhul-Hijjah . However, if you are staying over to pelt the Jamarāt on the 13th of Dhul-Hijjah as well, then you will need a total of 70 pebbles.

Extra pebbles should be collected in case you miss or have a doubt as to whether the pebble has landed in the right area or not, as you will have to pelt again.

Dates for Throwing Pebbles

10th Dhul-Hijjah - 7 pebbles
11th Dhul-Hijjah - 21 pebbles
12th Dhul-Hijjah - 21 pebbles
13th Dhul-Hijjah - 21 pebbles

Mas'alah
Collect the pebbles from a clean place so that you do not have to wash them. One should assume that the pebbles are clean if there are no signs of filth on them.

It is permissible to collect these pebbles from other places, not only from Muzdalifah.

Wuqoof (Stay) at Muzdalifah

Perform Fajr Salāh in Muzdalifah as soon as its time commences.
Note: A lot of people give the Adhān for Fajr Salāh and perform it before the beginning time of Fajr and leave immediately for Minā before Subha Sādiq. By doing this, they miss the Wuqoof of Muzdalifah (Wājib) which brings upon them the liability of Dam. Therefore, one should ensure that the Fajr Adhān time is noted in Makkah and approximately five minutes after this time, perform the Fajr Salāh.

Mas'alah

The Wuqoof of Muzdalifah is Wājib and its time commences from Subha Sādiq and ends at sunrise. If one spent even a little portion of this time in Muzdalifah, he will be absolved of this obligation. However, it is better to remain until just before sunrise.

Du'ā in Muzdalifah

It is Sunnah to make Du'ā in Muzdalifah after the Fajr Salāh. One Du'ā of our Holy Prophet ﷺ was not accepted in Arafāt but it was accepted here in Muzdalifah.

Mas'alah

The method of Du'ā should be exactly the same as that which was adopted in Arafāt. Facing the Qiblah remain engaged in worship until just before sunrise and continue reciting Talbiyah, Tasbeeh and supplicating to Allāh ﷻ.

Day 3 - 10th of Dhul-Hijjah

Back in Minā
Just before sunrise, you will leave for Minā reciting Talbiyah, Dhikr and Tasbeeh.

Note: There is no Eidul-Adhā Salāh upon the pilgrims on the 10th of Dhul-Hijjah.

On this 3rd day (10th of Dhul-Hijjah), there are four obligations to carry out. In fact, this is the most busiest day of Hajj comprising of many rituals. Hence, make sure all the rituals are carried out in the right manner.

1)   RAMEE - Pelting the big Jamarah (Shaytān). This is Wājib.
2)   NAHR - Animal sacrifice. This is Wājib.
3)   HALAQ or QASR - Shaving or trimming of the hair. This is Wājib.
4)   TAWAF-E-ZIYARĀT – This is Fardh.
*All these will be explained in the forthcoming pages

Mas'alah
For those pilgrims performing Hajj Qirān or Hajj Tamattu, it is Wājib to carry out the first three obligations above in order. Failure to do so will result in giving a Dam (penalty).

Mas'alah
If the sacrifice of an animal is carried out by an agent, the pilgrim should appoint a time and make sure the animal is sacrificed at the fixed time. If it is delayed or it has not been sacrificed at the appointed time and he gets his head shaved or hair trimmed, then a Dam will become due on him.

Mas'alah

It is Mustahab (desirable) for those performing Hajj Ifrād to have their sacrifice done and not Wājib. Therefore, they can shave or trim their hair as soon as they have completed their Ramee (pelting).

If the Mufrid (one who is performing Hajj Ifrād) wishes to fulfil the ritual of sacrifice, then he is at liberty to do so before or after the Halaq or Qasr. However, it is Mustahab (preferable) to follow the respective order for them too.

Ramee (Pelting)

Today, (the 10th of Dhul-Hijjah)one will only pelt the Jamarah Aqabah (big Shaytān).

Mas'alah

Ramee is Wājib. Failure to carry out the Ramee will result in paying a penalty.

Note: It is Bid'ah (innovation) to pelt the other two Jamarāt, Jamarah al-Wustā (medium Shaytān) and Jamarah as-Sugrā (small Shaytān).

Time for Ramee (Pelting)

The pelting time on the 10th of Dhul-Hijjah starts at the beginning time of Fajr Salāh and ends as soon as Fajr time (Subah Sādiq) starts on the 11th of Dhul-Hijjah.

Pelting is not allowed before the time of Fajr (Subah Sādiq).

- It is Makrooh from Subah Sādiq (beginning time of Fajr) till sunrise.
- It is Sunnat form sunrise to Zawāl.
- It is Mubāh (permissible) from Zawāl to sunset.
- It is Makrooh from sunset till the start of the time of Fajr Salāh on the 11th of Dhul-Hijjah .

Mas'alah

There is no Makrooh time for pelting for women, sick people and the disabled fearing the crowds. In fact, it is more virtuous for them to carry it out at night.

A word of caution...

Take extra care at the Jamarāt so that you do not get hit by pebbles. Protect and safeguard your face and keep your head low. Be careful that you do not get hurt on the face by the elbows of the pilgrims who are pelting.

Note:

One should try to pelt the Jamarāt in the Sunnat time or at least the Mubāh time. However, if there is large crowd or any difficulty, then it can be delayed until after Maghrib.

Method of Ramee

Proceed towards Jamarah-Aqabah (big Shaytān) and stand approximately 7.5 feet (2.5 yards) or more away from it. One will stand in such a way that the Minā Masjid (Masjid Khayf) is to your right and Makkah is to your left.

Throw seven pebbles, one at a time, with the index finger and the thumb of the right hand reciting بِسْمِ اللهِ اللهُ اَكْبَر - 'Bismillāhi Allāhu Akbar' each time.

Mas'alah
It is Sunnat to be in the state of Wudhu, however it is not Wājib.

Mas'alah
If you are left handed, try to make an effort to use the right hand as the Jamarāt are very big so the chances of missing are very low.

Mas'alah
If you pelt two or more pebbles at the same time into a pot, it will count as if you have only pelted one pebble.

Mas'alah
If the pebble hits the pillar and does not land in the pot, then it will not be valid, another pebble must be thrown.

Mas'alah
The Talbiyah will be stopped as soon as the first pebble lands in the pot.

Mas'alah
When pelting, raise the hands completely straight up so that your armpit becomes visible. This is the Sunnah method.

Note: There is no Du'ā after the Ramee of Jamarah-Aqabah (Big Shaytān).

Appointing a Proxy to Pelt

Pelting must be carried out in person. However, if a person is ill or so old that he performs his Salāh sitting down or is too weak to get to the Jamarāt, then he can allow someone to pelt on his behalf. Many people pelt on behalf of others without a genuine, valid Shar'ee excuse or reason. Remember, in such circumstances, the Ramee will be invalid and penalty will become compulsory.

Note: Crowds or rush is not a valid reason to appoint a proxy. Nowadays, pelting has become much easier due to the extension of the Jamarāt. The pots and pillars are much bigger than before with more floors to pelt from.

Mas'alah
The Sunnah method for the person who has been appointed a proxy is that he should pelt his pebbles first, then the pebbles of the ill or elderly person.

Nahr (Animal Sacrifice)

The second obligation for today is animal sacrifice. This sacrifice is known as Dam-e-Shukr and it is Wājib upon those performing Hajj Qirān and Hajj Tamattu and it is Mustahab for those who are performing Hajj Ifrād.

Mas'alah
The period of time for performing Dam-e-Shukr starts from after the Ramee until the sunset on the 12th of Dhul-Hijjah .

50

Eid Qurbāni and Hajj Qurbāni

Many people get confused between the Eid Qurbāni and Hajj Qurbāni. Remember that Hajj Qurbāni (Dam-e-Shukr) is only Wājib upon those performing Hajj Qirān or Hajj Tamattu. On the other hand, the Eid Qurbāni is Wājib annually upon every Muslim who is sane, Bāligh (physically mature) and upon whom Zakāt is Fardh (compulsory) and the person is not a Musāfir (Shar'ee traveler). During the days of Hajj, usually the pilgrim is a traveler (a person who has stayed less than 15 days in Makkah before leaving for Minā, as mentioned earlier in the chapter of Minā), thus it is not necessary to sacrifice, however it is desirable to do so.

Mas'alah
The annual Qurbāni can be done anywhere in the world. If you want, you may arrange the Qurbāni in your home town or in a needy part of the world before you leave home. This annual Qurbāni has no connection with Hajj and therefore, can be done anytime during the three days of Qurbāni.

Mas'alah
The pilgrim will need to make the Niyyat (intention) of sacrifice for Hajj Qirān or Hajj Tamattu or else the sacrifice will not be valid.

Mas'alah
It is more rewardable and virtuous to slaughter the animal oneself. If you are unable to do so, then it is Mustahab (recommended) to be present at the time of sacrifice. It is also Mustahab to partake from its meat.

Halaq/Qasr (Shaving and Trimming)

Once the sacrifice is completed, the pilgrim should shave or trim his hair. He should sit facing the Qiblah and start the shaving from the right hand side. Whilst the Halaq or Qasr is taking place, the pilgrim should recite Takbeer and engage in supplications.

Mas'alah
Women will take the tip of the plait of their hair and cut one inch. If the hair is very fine at the tip of the plait, then that tip should be ignored and the inch for cutting should be measured from further up the plait. If the hair is very short (e.g. only up to the neck), the woman should still cut an inch of the hair to leave the state of Ihrām.

Note: The hair must not be cut in Safā or Marwah as the hair will fall in the areas around Masjid-Harām and non Mahrams will see the hair.

Mas'alah
Shaving for men is more virtuous than trimming. The Holy Prophet ﷺ made Du'ā thrice for those who shaved their hair. Remember it is Harām for women to shave their heads.

Mas'alah
The period of time fixed for cutting the hair for both men and women (performing Hajj Qirān or Hajj Tamattu) starts after the sacrifice has been completed and the time will remain until the sunset on 12th of Dhul-Hijjah. The Mufrid (pilgrim performing only Hajj) may cut his or her hair straight after pelting the big Jamarah on the 10th of Dhul-Hijjah . The ending time for a Mufrid is the same as the Qārin and Mutamatti.

Women in the state of menstruation must also cut their hair.

Mas'alah
If the cutting of the hair is delayed until after sunset on the 12th of Dhul-Hijjah , it will be a sin and will also result in a penalty (Dam).

The hair must be cut in any part of the Haram. This includes Makkah, Minā and Muzdalifah. Otherwise, it will be a sin to cut outside the Harām e.g. Jeddah or Madeenah and will also result in a penalty. To cut the hair in Minā is Sunnah.

Mas'alah
It is Wājib to shave or trim a quarter of ones head to come out of Ihrām and to shave or trim the whole head is Sunnah. However, to shave or trim only a quarter or have short back and sides is prohibited.

Mas'alah
If the pilgrim has completed all the rites of Hajj which he had to perform before Halaq, then he can himself shave his head and he can also shave or trim another pilgrim's hair.

Note: Once the hair has been cut, all the restrictions of Ihrām are uplifted, such as using soap and shampoo, except for sexual relations. This final restriction of the Ihrām (marital relations) will only be lifted once Tawāf-e-Ziyārat is complete.

Tawāf-e-Ziyārat

Now you will proceed to Makkah to perform Tawāf-e-Ziyārat.

Time for Tawāf-e-Ziyārat

The time for performing Tawāf-e-Ziyārat starts from the beginning time of Fajr Salāh on the 10th of Dhul-Hijjah and remains until the sunset on the 12th of Dhul-Hijjah. This time is fixed for all three types of Hajj.

Mas'alah

It is Wājib to perform Tawāf-e-Ziyārat before the sunset of the 12th of Dhul-Hijjah. A delay will result in Dam. A woman in the state of menstruation must delay her Tawāf-e-Ziyārat until she becomes pure. In this case, there is no Dam upon her.

Mas'alah

If Sa'ee has already been performed after Tawāf-e-Qudoom by those performing Hajj Qirān and Hajj Ifrād or after putting on an Ihrām for Hajj (by those performing Hajj Tamattu), then one does not need to perform the Sa'ee again and the Tawāf will be done without Ramal or Idhtibā.

However, if Sa'ee is yet to be performed, then one should do Ramal in the first three rounds and if wearing the Ihrām, the Idhtibā in all seven rounds.

Mas'alah

Tawāf-e-Ziyārat may be performed before or after Ramee, sacrifice or shaving. However, it is Sunnah to perform it after Halaq or Qasr.

54

Mas'alah

It is Sunnah to have a bath or shower before performing Tawāf-e-Ziyārat.

Note: Tawāf-e-Ziyārat is Fardh, therefore Hajj will remain incomplete without it. A woman in the state of menstruation may delay Tawāf-e-Ziyārat but it will not be waived from her. If she returns home without performing Tawāf-e-Ziyārat, her Hajj will remain incomplete and sexual relations will remain unlawful until she returns to Makkah and performs Tawāf-e-Ziyārat, irrespective of the time limit.

If the woman is not married, she may marry but marital relations with the husband will remain unlawful until after the Tawāf-e-Ziyārat. The same rule applies to a man if he has not performed Tawāf-e-Ziyārat, that it will not be lawful for him to have relations with his wife.

Mas'alah

After completing the seven circuits of Tawāf-e-Ziyārat, perform two Ra-k'ats of Tawāf Salāh. If Sa'ee wasn't performed earlier, then perform Sa'ee after the Tawāf and then proceed to Minā.

Spending Nights in Minā After The Tawāf-e-Ziyārat

The nights of the 10th and 11th Dhul-Hijjah should be spent in Minā. The importance of this Sunnah of spending the nights in Minā can be realized from the juristic rulings that besides the Hanafi school of thought, the other three, namely Māliki, Shāfiee and Hanbali, are all of the opinion that spending the nights of the 10th and 11th in Minā is necessary and that not to do so will be a sin and will also result in a penalty.

Do not stay in the hotels in Makkah due to laziness. Remember, you are not here on a holiday, you have to make an effort to get back to Minā. Many people discard this practice of the Holy Prophet ﷺ. The nights spent in Minā are a lot more virtuous than the luxurious hotels of Makkah.

Day 4 - 11th Dhul-Hijjah

On this day, the pelting of all three Jamarāt is necessary. You will throw seven pebbles separately at each of the three Jamarāt known as Jamarah Sugrā (small Shaytān), Jamarah Wustā (middle Shaytān) and Jamarah Aqabah (big Shaytān).

Time for Ramee

The time for Ramee on the 11th and 12th of Dhul-Hijjah begins at Zawāl (midday) and ends at Subha Sādiq the following morning.

Note: It is not allowed to pelt before midday. If it is done before this time, it must be repeated. Not to repeat it will be a sin and will also result in a penalty.

Sunnah Time to Pelt

The Sunnah time to pelt is from Zawāl to sunset. Try and pelt at this time provided you are certain that you will not get caught up in the crowd. Avoid congestion and intense crowd at all times.

Makrooh Time

The Makrroh time to pelt is from sunset to Subha Sādiq. It is disliked for men but the pelting will be valid. It is not Makrooh for women, the elderly and the sick. If the husband/Mahram needs to be with a woman who will be pelting at this time, he should pelt at this time as well. In this case, it will not be disliked for him to pelt.

Pelting the Three Jamarāt

It is Sunnah to pelt seven pebbles in the small Jamarah first, the one closest to Masjid-e-Khaif, then the medium Jamarah and finally, the big Jamarah.

If the pelting is carried out in the wrong order, it does not need to be re-peated and will not result in a penalty.

The method of Ramee has already been mentioned in the chapter 'Third day - 10th Dhul-Hijjah.' Please refer to that chapter.

Du'ā After Pelting the First two Jamarāt

After pelting the small and the medium Jamarāt, it is Sunnah to face the Qiblah and make Du'ā for a short while with your hands raised. It is not Sunnah to make Du'ā after pelting the big Jamarah. You will pelt the big Jamarah and move on. This method of Du'ā will be adopted on all the days of pelting.

Note: After pelting, immediately return to your camp if you have performed your Tawāf-e-Ziyārat. Do not waste time as many people do during the days of Hajj.

Day 5 -12th Dhul-Hijjah

On this day, like the previous day, the pelting of all three Jamarāt is neces-sary. The pelting time on the 12th of Dhul-Hijjah is exactly like the previ-ous day. Pelting time starts after Zawāl (mid-day) and ends at Subah Sādiq (beginning time of Fajr Salāh the next day). Remember, pelting before Zawāl on this day is also not permissible.

A Misunderstanding and the Clarification

It is commonly misunderstood amongst people that one must leave the boundary of Minā before sunset on the 12th of Dhul-Hijjah, otherwise it will be necessary to pelt on the 13th of Dhul-Hijjah. This is not correct. The correct ruling is that it is permissible to leave for Makkah even after sunset on the 12th of Dhul-Hijjah without having to stay to pelt on the 13th of Dhul-Hijjah .

The pelting on the 13th of Dhul-Hijjah will only be necessary if one is present in Minā at Subah Sādiq.

Many people, due to this misunderstanding try to leave Minā before sun-set and in their endeavor, they either pelt the Jamarāt before Zawāl which is invalid or they wait in the scorching heat before Zawāl, so that they can pelt as soon as the time enters. In this way, they are harming themselves as well as other pilgrims.

Note: Remember to perform your Maghrib Salāh on time. Many pil-grims on their way back to Makkah are held up in crowds or traffic jams and do not perform Maghrib Salāh. Perform it before it becomes Qadhā wherever you are and perform Ishā Salāh once you have returned to Mak-kah.

Day 6 - 13th Dhul-Hijjah

It is Mustahab (desirable) to pelt on this day and not Wājib (necessary). Remember, it is more virtuous and of greater merit to pelt all the three Jamarāt on the 13th of Dhul-Hijjah as well.

For those pilgrims who have chosen to pelt the Jamarāt on the 13th also, then they should follow the same procedure mentioned on the 11th or 12th of Dhul-Hijjah .

The time for Ramee (pelting) will be as follows:

• From Subha Sādiq to Zawāl - Makrooh
• From Zawāl to sunset - Masnoon.

Note: The time for pelting on the 13th of Dhul-Hijjah ends immediately at sunset. If the pelting is not completed by then, it will be a sin and also result in a Dam (penalty).

Mas'alah
Takbeer Tashreeq will be recited for the last time after the Asr Salāh on the 13th of Dhul-Hijjah .

Tawāf-e-Widā (Farewell Tawāf)

Tawāf-e-Widā is the farewell Tawāf which can be performed anytime after Tawāf-e-Ziyārat but it is most desirable to perform it just before leaving Makkah. Tawāf-e-Widā is Wājib on the pilgrim. Any Tawāf performed after Tawāf-e-Ziyārat will be counted as Tawāf-e-Widā even though the intention of Tawāf-e-Widā was not made or an intention of Nafl Tawāf was made.

Mas'alah

Before Tawāf-e-Widā, there is no need to enter into Ihrām nor is there any Sa'ee after the Tawāf or cutting of the hair. The two Rak'āts of Tawāf will be performed as normal.

Mas'alah

A woman who is in her menstruation does not need to wait for her menstruation to end to perform the Tawāf-e-Widā, she may return home without performing it.

Mas'alah

If a person does not perform Tawāf-e-Widā, then he will be liable for Dam. If a woman was not in her menstruation before leaving Makkah and leaves without performing any Tawāf after Tawāf-e-Ziyārat, this will be a sin and will also result in a penalty.

Note: It is a common misconception that after Tawāf-e-Widā, a person cannot enter the Haram or perform Tawāf. This is not so. A person is allowed to continue to perform Salāh in the Masjid Harām and perform Nafl Tawāf or Umrah.

Alhamdulillāh, by the grace of Allāh ﷻ, all the rituals of Hajj are now complete. May Allāh ﷻ accept your Hajj and fulfill all your needs.

Please remember the humble author and his family and all those who contributed in making this publication possible in your Du'ās. Āmeen.

61

Ziyārat of Madeenah Munawwarah

The Holy Prophet ﷺ has said, "Whoever visits me after my death is like he who visited me during my lifetime." (Dārul Qutni)

In another narration it says, "For whoever visits my grave, my intercession becomes obligatory." (Bazzār)

It is permissible to perform Ziyārat before or after Hajj. Ziyārat is to present oneself in the sacred court of the beloved Prophet ﷺ, in other words, to visit the Rawdah (grave of the blessed Prophet ﷺ). When one is about to embark on the journey of Madeenah Munawwarah, he should make the intention of visiting the sacred grave as well as Masjid Nabawi.

Whilst travelling towards Madeenah Munawwarah, take special precaution in practicing upon all the Sunnats and reciting Durood Shareef in abundance. When you have reached your destination, adhere to your needs and then prepare for your Ziyārat. Have a shower or at least perform Wudhu. Thereafter, wear the best clothes you have. Men should apply sweet smelling perfume. After entering the Masjid, perform two Rak'āts Tahiyyatul Masjid.

Note: Women are only allowed to come to the Rawdha (holy grave) at fixed times. Find out from the tour operator or those who have come before regarding the gate number and times for the Ziyārat for women.

At the Holy Grave

After performing Tahiyyatul Masjid, proceed towards the Rawdha with all thoughts immersed on the personality of the beloved Prophet ﷺ.

Note: When a person is facing the grave of the beloved Prophet ﷺ, there are three gold wire-mesh enclosures. There are round holes in all these three enclosures. Most people think that the beloved Prophet ﷺ is resting inside the first enclosure, Sayyidunā Abū Bakr ؓ in the second enclosure and Sayyidunā Umar ؓ in the third one. This is not so. They are all resting inside the second enclosure. There are three round holes in the middle enclosure while only two holes on the left and the right enclosures. The first hole in the middle enclosure (which is the largest of all) directly faces the holy face of the beloved Prophet ﷺ. Moving slightly to the right is the second hole (of the middle enclosure) which directs to the face of Sayyidunā Abū Bakr ؓ. Likewise, a third hole on this enclosure marks the spot where the face of Sayyidunā Umar ؓ rests.

Stand three or four paces away from the wire-mesh enclosure facing the holy grave with your back towards the Qiblah and with utmost humility recite Salām in a moderate tone, not too softly nor too loudly.

اَلصَّلٰوةُ وَالسَّلَامُ عَلَيْكَ يَا رَسُوْلَ اللّٰهِ

Assalātu Wassalāmu Alaika Yā Rasūlallāh

"May peace and salutations be upon you, O' Messenger of Allāh."

You may recite in any other words you wish as long as the words convey respect and honour.

63

Do not raise your hands whilst making Du'ā facing the Rawdha.

After having recited the Salām, convey the Salām of those who have asked you to convey their greetings to the Holy Prophet ﷺ.

The method will be like this:

**"Peace and Salutations be upon you, O' Messenger of Allāh ﷺ   from (the name of the person).
He requests you to intercede to your Lord on his behalf."**

Note: The humble author earnestly requests you to remember at the Rawdha to say Salām and Salutations on his behalf.

After sending salutations to the blessed Prophet ﷺ, move towards the right and recite greetings to Sayyidunā Abū Bakr ؓ.

اَلسَّلاَمُ عَلَيْكَ يَا خَلِيْفَةَ رَسُوْلِ اللهِ جَزَاكَ اللهُ عَنْ اُمَّةِ مُحَمَّدٍ صَلَّى اللهُ عَلَيْهِ وَسَلَّمُ

"Peace be upon you, O' Caliph of the Holy Prophet ﷺ. May Allāh ﷻ reward you well on behalf of the Ummah of Muhammad ﷺ."

Thereafter, move one more step to the right and recite greeting to Sayyidunā Umar ؓ saying,

اَلسَّلاَمُ عَلَيْكَ يَا اَمِيْرَ الْمُؤْمِنِيْنَ جَزَاكَ اللهُ عَنْ اُمَّةِ مُحَمَّدٍ صَلَّى اللهُ عَلَيْهِ وَسَلَّمُ

"Peace be upon you, O' Leader of the Believers. May Allāh ﷻ reward you well on behalf of the Ummah of Muhammad ﷺ."

After the Ziyārat, face the Qiblah and make Du'ā for yourself, your parents, family, relatives, teachers, students, friends, well-wishers and the Ummah of the beloved Prophet ﷺ.

Please remember this sinful servant, Saiful Islām in your accepted prayers. Āmeen!

May Allāh ﷻ accept your Ziyārat. May He bless us with the Ziyārat again and again. Āmeen!

Bibliography

The Holy Qur' ān

Saheeh al-Bukhāri - by Imām Muhammad Ibn Ismā'eel al-Bukhāri ﷺ

Mishkātul Masābeeh – by Allāmah Baghawi ﷺ

Hidāyah - by Imām Burhānudeen Marghināni ﷺ

Mukhtasarul Qudoori - by Imām Abul Husain al-Qudoori al-Baghdādi ﷺ

Nurul Iydhāh - by Imām Hasan Shurunbulāli ﷺ

The priceless Gift of Hajj - by Shaykhul Hadeeth Maulanā Muslihuddin Ahmad

A Woman's Guide to Hajj and Umrah - by Mufti Muhammad Farooq

How To Perform Hajj - by Shaykh Muhammad Saleem Dhorāt

How to Perform Umrah - by Shaykh Muhammad Saleem Dhorāt

Mu'allimul Hujjāj - Maulanā Sa'eed Ahmad

Fazāil-Hajj—Shaykhul Hadeeth Maulanā Muhammad Zakariyyah ﷺ

How May Women Perform Hajj - by Mufti Abdur Rauf Sakharvi

Hajj the Fifth Pillar of Islām - by Shaykh Mūsā Ibrāhim Menk

Kitābul Umrah - Mufti Muhammad Āshiq Ilāhi Bulandshahri ﷺ

Other titles from JKN Publications

Your Questions Answered

An outstanding book written by Shaykh Mufti Saiful Islām. A very comprehensive yet simple Fatāwa book and a source of guidance that reaches out to a wider audience i.e. the English speaking Muslims. The reader will benefit from the various answers to questions based on the Laws of Islām relating to the beliefs of Islām, knowledge, Sunnah, pillars of Islām, marriage, divorce and contemporary issues.

UK RRP: £7.50

Hadeeth for Beginners

A concise Hadeeth book with various Ahādeeth that relate to basic Ibādāh and moral etiquettes in Islām accessible to a wider readership. Each Hadeeth has been presented with the Arabic text, its translation and commentary to enlighten the reader, its meaning and application in day-to-day life.

UK RRP: £3.00

Du'ā for Beginners

This book contains basic Du'ās which every Muslim should recite on a daily basis. Highly recommended to young children and adults studying at Islamic schools and Madrasahs so that one may cherish the beautiful treasure of supplications of our beloved Prophet ﷺ in one's daily life, which will ultimately bring peace and happiness in both worlds, Inshā-Allāh.

UK RRP: £2.00

How well do you know Islām?

An exciting educational book which contains 300 multiple questions and answers to help you increase your knowledge on Islām! Ideal for the whole family, especially children and adult students to learn new knowledge in an enjoyable way and cherish the treasures of knowledge that you will acquire from this book. A very beneficial tool for educational syllabus.

UK RRP: £3.00

Treasures of the Holy Qur'ān

This book entitled "Treasures of the Holy Qur'ān" has been compiled to create a stronger bond between the Holy Qur'ān and the readers. It mentions the different virtues of Sūrahs and verses from the Holy Qur'ān with the hope that the readers will increase their zeal and enthusiasm to recite and inculcate the teachings of the Holy Qur'ān into their daily lives.

UK RRP: £3.00

Other titles from JKN PUBLICATIONS

Marriage - A Complete Solution

Islām regards marriage as a great act of worship. This book has been designed to provide the fundamental teachings and guidelines of all what relates to the marital life in a simplified English language. It encapsulates in a nutshell all the marriage laws mentioned in many of the main reference books in order to facilitate their understanding and implementation.

UK RRP: £5.00

Pearls of Luqmān

This book is a comprehensive commentary of Sūrah Luqmān, written beautifully by Shaykh Mufti Saiful Islām. It offers the reader with an enquiring mind, abundance of advice, guidance, counselling and wisdom.

The reader will be enlightened by many wonderful topics and anecdotes mentioned in this book, which will create a greater understanding of the Holy Qur'ān and its wisdom. The book highlights some of the wise sayings and words of advice Luqmān ﷺ gave to his son.

UK RRP: £3.00

Arabic Grammar for Beginners

This book is a study of Arabic Grammar based on the subject of Nahw (Syntax) in a simplified English format. If a student studies this book thoroughly, he/she will develop a very good foundation in this field, Inshā-Allāh. Many books have been written on this subject in various languages such as Arabic, Persian and Urdu. However, in this day and age there is a growing demand for this subject to be available in English .

UK RRP: £3.00

A Gift to My Youngsters

This treasure filled book, is a collection of Islamic stories, morals and anecdotes from the life of our beloved Prophet ﷺ, his Companions ﷺ and the pious predecessors. The stories and anecdotes are based on moral and ethical values, which the reader will enjoy sharing with their peers, friends, families and loved ones.

"A Gift to My Youngsters" – is a wonderful gift presented to the readers personally, by the author himself, especially with the youngsters in mind. He has carefully selected stories and anecdotes containing beautiful morals, lessons and valuable knowledge and wisdom.

UK RRP: £5.00

Travel Companion

The beauty of this book is that it enables a person on any journey, small or distant or simply at home, to utilise their spare time to read and benefit from an exciting and vast collection of important and interesting Islamic topics and lessons. Written in simple and easy to read text, this book will immensely benefit both the newly interested person in Islām and the inquiring mind of a student expanding upon their existing knowledge. Inspiring reminders from the Holy Qur'ān and the blessed words of our beloved Prophet ﷺ beautifies each topic and will illuminate the heart of the reader.   **UK RRP: £5.00**

Pearls of Wisdom

Junaid Baghdādi ﷺ once said, "Allāh ﷻ strengthens through these Islamic stories the hearts of His friends, as proven from the Qur'anic verse, **"And all that We narrate unto you of the stories of the Messengers, so as to strengthen through it your heart."** (11:120)
Mālik Ibn Dinār ﷺ stated that such stories are gifts from Paradise. He also emphasised to narrate these stories as much as possible as they are gems and it is possible that an individual might find a truly rare and invaluable gem among them.   **UK RRP: £6.00**

Inspirations

This book contains a compilation of selected speeches delivered by Shaykh Mufti Saiful Islām on a variety of topics such as the Holy Qur'ān, Nikāh and eating Halāl. Having previously been compiled in separate booklets, it was decided that the transcripts be gathered together in one book for the benefit of the reader. In addition to this, we have included in this book, further speeches which have not yet been printed.

UK RRP: £6.00

Gift to my Sisters

A thought provoking compilation of very interesting articles including real life stories of pious predecessors, imaginative illustrations and much more. All designed to influence and motivate mothers, sisters, wives and daughters towards an ideal Islamic lifestyle. A lifestyle referred to by our Creator, Allāh ﷻ in the Holy Qur'ān as the means to salvation and ultimate success.

UK RRP: £6.00

Gift to my Brothers

A thought provoking compilation of very interesting articles including real life stories of pious predecessors, imaginative illustrations, medical advices on intoxicants and rehabilitation and much more. All designed to influence and motivate fathers, brothers, husbands and sons towards an ideal Islamic lifestyle. A lifestyle referred to by our Creator, Allāh ﷻ in the Holy Qur'ān as the means to salvation and ultimate success.

UK RRP: £5.00

Heroes of Islām

"In the narratives there is certainly a lesson for people of intelligence (understanding)." (12:111)

A fine blend of Islamic personalities who have been recognised for leaving a lasting mark in the hearts and minds of people.

A distinguishing feature of this book is that the author has selected not only some of the most world and historically famous renowned scholars but also these lesser known and a few who have simply left behind a valuable piece of advice to their nearest and dearest. **UK RRP: £5.00**

Ask a Mufti (3 volumes)

Muslims in every generation have confronted different kinds of challenges. In-spite of that, Islām produced such luminary Ulamā who confronted and re-sponded to the challenges of their time to guide the Ummah to the straight path. "Ask A Mufti" is a comprehensive three volume fatwa book, based on the Hanafi School, covering a wide range of topics related to every aspect of human life such as belief, ritual worship, life after death and contemporary legal topics related to purity, commercial transaction, marriage, divorce, food, cosmetic, laws pertaining to women, Islamic medical ethics and much more.

UK RRP: £30.00

Should I Follow a Madhab?

Taqleed or following one of the four legal schools is not a new phenomenon. Historically, scholars of great calibre and luminaries, each one being a specialist in his own right, were known to have adhered to one of the four legal schools. It is only in the previous century that a minority group emerged advocating a se-vere ban on following one of the four major schools.

This book endeavours to address the topic of Taqleed and elucidates its im-portance and necessity in this day and age. It will also, by the Divine Will of Allāh ﷻ dispel some of the confusion surrounding this topic. **UK RRP: £5.00**

Advice for the Students of Knowledge

Allāh ﷻ describes divine knowledge in the Holy Qur'ān as a 'Light'. Amongst the qualities of light are purity and guidance. The Holy Prophet ﷺ has clearly ex-plained this concept in many blessed Ahādeeth and has also taught us many supplications in which we ask for beneficial knowledge.

This book is a golden tool for every sincere student of knowledge wishing to mould his/her character and engrain those correct qualities in order to be wor-thy of receiving the great gift of Ilm from Allāh ﷻ. **UK RRP: £3.00**

Stories for Children

"Stories for Children" - is a wonderful gift presented to the readers personally by the author himself, especially with the young children in mind. The stories are based on moral and ethical values, which the reader will enjoy sharing with their peers, friends, families and loved ones. The aim is to present to the children stories and incidents which contain moral lessons, in order to reform and correct their lives, according to the Holy Qur'ān and Sunnah.

UK RRP: £5.00

Pearls from My Shaykh

This book contains a collection of pearls and inspirational accounts of the Holy Prophet 鐃, his noble Companions, pious predecessors and some personal accounts and sayings of our well-known contemporary scholar and spiritual guide, Shaykh Mufti Saiful Islām Sāhib. Each anecdote and narrative of the pious predecessors have been written in the way that was narrated by Mufti Saiful Islām Sāhib in his discourses, drawing the specific lessons he intended from telling the story. The accounts from the life of the Shaykh has been compiled by a particular student based on their own experience and personal observation. **UK RRP: £5.00**

Paradise & Hell

This book is a collection of detailed explanation of Paradise and Hell including the state and conditions of its inhabitants. All the details have been taken from various reliable sources. The purpose of its compilation is for the reader to contemplate and appreciate the innumerable favours, rewards, comfort and unlimited luxuries of Paradise and at the same time take heed from the punishment of Hell. Shaykh Mufti Saiful Islām Sāhib has presented this book in a unique format by including the Tafseer and virtues of Sūrah Ar-Rahmān. **UK RRP: £5.00**

Prayers for Forgiveness

Prayers for Forgiveness' is a short compilation of Du'ās in Arabic with English translation and transliteration. This book can be studied after 'Du'ā for Beginners' or as a separate book. It includes twenty more Du'ās which have not been mentioned in the previous Du'ā book. It also includes a section of Du'ās from the Holy Qur'ān and a section from the Ahādeeth. The book concludes with a section mentioning the Ninety-Nine Names of Allāh 鐃 with its translation and transliteration. **UK RRP: £3.00**

Scattered Pearls

This book is a collection of scattered pearls taken from books, magazines, emails and WhatsApp messages. These pearls will hopefully increase our knowledge, wisdom and make us realise the purpose of life. In this book, Mufti Sāhib has included messages sent to him from scholars, friends and colleagues which will be beneficial and interesting for our readers Inshā-Allāh. **UK RRP: £4.00**

Poems of Wisdom

This book is a collection of poems from those who contributed to the Al-Mumin Magazine in the poems section. The Hadeeth mentions "Indeed some form of poems are full of wisdom." The themes of each poem vary between wittiness, thought provocation, moral lessons, emotional to name but a few. The readers will benefit from this immensely and make them ponder over the outlook of life in general.

UK RRP: £4.00